The Psychology Of Sin

James H. Snowden

KESSINGER
PUBLISHING

CHAPTER IV

THE PSYCHOLOGY OF SIN

THE natural and primal relation of man to God, we must believe, was one of harmony in which filial love and obedience blended with paternal love and care into fellowship. Historically in the beginning of the race this fellowship may have been only germinal, but it contained no seeds of discord. But something happened that broke this harmony and shattered all the music of the world. The world bears universal and abundant witness that it is out of joint, a mass of wounds and woe, a scene of discord and strife. At some point a serpent crept into its garden and poisoned its life; on some fatal day occurred

> Man's disobedience and the fruit
> Of that forbidden tree, whose mortal taste
> Brought death into the world, and all our woe.

We are concerned, however, not with the historical and theological problems, but only with the psychological nature and operations, of sin. All the way through our subject, psychology deals with religion mainly on its human and subjective side; its divine objective side falls within the field of theology.

I. The Nature of Sin

1. **The Biblical Idea of Sin.**—There are three leading words used in the Old Testament and three in the New that express the Biblical idea of sin.

(*a*) The Hebrew words are translated sin, iniquity and transgression, and they are all found in one verse, Ex. 34: 7: "keeping lovingkindness for thousands, forgiving iniquity and transgression and sin." The word translated sin, *chattath*,[1] expresses "sin as *missing one's aim*. The etymology does not suggest a person against whom the sin is committed, and does not necessarily imply intentional wrongdoing. But the use of the word is not limited by its etymology, and the sin may be against man (Gen. 40: 1, I Sam. 30: 1) or against God (Ex. 32: 33)."[2]

The word translated iniquity, *avon*,[3] means "literally 'perversion,' 'distortion.' It is to be distinguished from *chattath*[1] as being a quality of actions rather than an act, and it thus acquires the sense of guilt. Guilt may be described as the sinner's position in regard to God which results from his sin." This Hebrew word and idea of sin is closely paralleled by our English word "wrong," which is only another spelling of the word "wrung," and represents wrong as that which is wrung out of its proper shape, or out of conformity to that which is right or straight.

The word translated transgression, *pesha*,[4] expresses "a breaking away from a law or covenant, and thus implies a law and lawgiver. It implies what *chattath*[1] does not necessarily imply, namely, the voluntariness of sin."

(*b*) The Greek words for sin in the New Testa-

[1] חַטָּאת.

[2] This and other quotations in this connection are taken from Hastings' *Dictionary of the Bible*, article Sin.

[3] עָוֹן. [4] פֶּשַׁע.

ment exactly parallel these Hebrew words in meaning.

The word translated sin, *hamartia*,[1] like *chattath*,[2] means missing the mark and may "mean sin as a habit, a state, a power, and also a single act of sin."

The word translated iniquity, *anomia*,[3] literally means lawlessness or anarchy. "In its strict sense it truly represents the conception of sin given in the Epistles of James and John." "Sin is lawlessness" (*anomia*). I John 3:4.

The word translated transgression, *parabasis*,[4] literally means transgressing and presupposes "the existence of a law."

These Biblical words for sin thus mean missing the mark, the mark of worth and duty that one should aim at and falling below it or going beside it to some lower or other end; twisting and perverting character and conduct into a crooked thing; and transgressing the law. These ideas all imply a standard or scale of values that should be conformed to and make sin consist in missing, perverting, and transgressing it.

These ideas also all imply and run up into the idea of God as the highest mark and ultimate standard or law that one should attain. At times this final incidence and guilt of sin is in the background of consciousness, and at other times it becomes intense as the central hot spot of consciousness, as in David's cry, "Against thee, thee only have I sinned (*chata*), and done this evil in thy sight" (Ps. 51:4), though the first incidence of his sin in this case was against a fellow-man. Any violation of the moral

[1] ἁμαρτία. [2] חַטָּאת [3] ἀνομία. [4] παράβασις.

law is on its human side a wrong deed or, in the case of the violation of civil law, a crime, but viewed in its relation to God's law it is a sin. All crimes are sins, but all sins are not crimes.

The Biblical idea of sin is succinctly expressed in the definition of the Westminster Shorter Catechism: "Sin is any want of conformity unto or transgression of the law of God."

2. The Psychological Nature of Sin.—We have already unfolded the psychological nature of sin as a wrong choice between a higher and a lower order of worth and obligation on the scale of value. This scale has as its highest point and final standard the worth and wisdom and will of God. Any choice of a lower in the presence of a higher good is a missing of the mark, a perversion or twisting of the right and a transgression of that law. As God's wisdom and will run down through the whole scale, any such act of wrong choice is explicit or implicit rebellion against him and is sin.

The deeper question now arises as to the essence of sin. Wherein does its essential principle consist? What is the tap root that sprouts into all its scarlet blossoms and bitter fruits? The question runs into philosophy, but it also pertains to psychology. There are three leading theories on this subject which call for attention.[1]

(*a*) The first theory is that sin is sensuousness. It is due to our animal heredity and the survival in us of brute instincts and passions. It is of the nature of a physical disorder and disease. It is rooted in the blood

[1] For a full discussion of these theories, see Dr. Augustus H. Strong's *Systematic Theology*, Vol. II, pp. 559-573, and Julius Müller, *The Christian Doctrine of Sin*, Vol. I, pp. 25-203.

and is a bondage into which we are born and from which we cannot escape.

There is an element of truth in this theory. Many of the coarser sins of the soul, such as gluttony and intemperance, ally themselves with the flesh and express themselves in and through the body. The term "flesh" in the New Testament means the carnal or fleshly nature of the soul, or the soul as allied with and rooted in the body. The soul uses the body as the instrument of many of its sins, and leaves deposits of its sins in the tissues and habits of the body until it becomes soaked and saturated with evil.

Yet this element of truth in it being granted, the main contention of the theory as to the essential nature of sin cannot be accepted. It roots evil in a material organism and is allied to the old Manichean theory that matter is essentially evil in nature. Matter in itself is neither moral nor immoral, for it has no ethical element in its constitution.

The animal also is below the plane of personal being and has no moral character. Granting that man did derive his bodily organism through evolution, yet the animal nature in the animal was not evil or in any degree moral, and therefore could not have transmitted any evil to man. The instincts and passions of man, however they may have been derived from a lower origin, did not become perverted and evil until man made them so. And further, many sins have only the slightest connection with the body. The spiritual sins of pride, envy, malice, unbelief and enmity against God are the most heinous and the deadliest, and yet they cannot be blamed on the blood. The soul cannot point to the body, as Adam pointed to Eve, saying "She did it," and say, "The beast in me did it." Conscience contradicts this doctrine and fastens the guilt and essence of sin on the soul itself. If this theory is true the soul does not need a Saviour, but only the body needs a physician. The cure for sin is a cleansing of the blood.

(*b*) A second theory of the nature of sin is that it is due to our human finiteness. It is a necessary correlative of our finite moral nature as our ignorance is of our finite intellect. There is no escaping ignorance because every problem solved starts a hundred others that are not solved, and thus our ignorance, so to speak, grows faster than our knowledge. However vast the circle of our light, vaster still is the outlying circle of darkness which hems the light in. So our sin is the necessary shadow that attends our finite moral nature and we never can outgrow it or leap away from it. "Upon this view," says Dr. Strong, "sin is the blundering of inexperience, the thoughtlessness that takes evil for good, the ignorance that puts its finger into the fire, the stumbling without which one cannot learn to walk. It is a fruit which is sour and bitter simply because it is immature. It is a means of discipline and training for something better,—it is holiness in the germ, good in the making." This is the view of Royce that "Evil is discord necessary to perfect harmony"; and of Browning:

> The evil is null, is naught, is silence implying sound;
> What was good shall be good, with, for evil, so much good more.

This view also contains an element of truth, for sin is connected with our finiteness and could not exist in an infinite being; and it is often turned to good in God's grace. But the fallacy of the view is that it confuses the imperfection of the finite with the fault and guilt of sin. It is no sin that we cannot be omniscient or that we cannot be perfect as the Infinite is perfect. Imperfection becomes sin only when it is evil in its nature.

The radical objection to this view is that it makes sin a necessary condition and activity of the soul, and it is therefore deterministic and pantheistic. In so doing it does what all determinism and pantheism do, it reduces morality to mechanism, ethics to physics, and thereby destroys its moral nature. When freedom is gone, no moral quality remains. Human wrongdoing is as necessary and unethical as the rain or wind. Such a theory explains sin by explaining it away and cutting it up by the roots, and all conscience and judgment and history unite to deny and condemn it.

(*c*) A third theory of sin is that it is essentially selfishness. Selfishness is to be distinguished from that self-love which is self-respect, appreciation, and affirmation of one's own worth and dignity and even rights. Such love of self is proper and necessary, for worth in the self has the same value and rights that it has in others; and unless one appreciates, develops, and guards his own worth he has nothing with which to love others. The command to "love thy neighbour as thyself" enjoins the love of self as the prior ground and means of loving one's neighbour.

But selfishness is a perversion of self-love and consists in putting the interests and possessions, pleasures and passions of the self in the centre and on the throne as the supreme principle of life. It subordinates other persons to its service as mere means to its own end; weaves other lives as threads into its own web; makes the soul wholly absorbent, so that it is a sponge sucking up everything and creating a desert around it, instead of being a fountain flinging forth streams refreshing and fertilizing other lives.

Selfishness is the essence of sin because it always chooses a lower good on the scale of value and obligation rather than a higher and the highest good, which is the perfection of social life and the perfect life of God. In thus choosing his own will man rebels against God. And it is the essence of sin because every kind of sin is a form of selfishness. The sins of the body, such as gluttony and intemperance, are all forms of personal gratification. Falsehood and dishonesty are obviously forms of selfishness. And the more spiritual sins of avarice, ambition, envy, jealousy, pride, and vanity are equally of the same nature. The most intellectual unbelief may involve a subtle element of pride of opinion and secret reluctance to obey the truth and thereby has a core of selfishness at its heart. In all their sins men miss the true mark because they aim at a lower mark of their own choosing; they pervert the right and transgress the law of God because they are seeking their own will and pleasure. It is human selfishness, then, in all its myriad manifestations and degrees, dim-eyed and blind or keen and cunning in its purpose, feeble or enormous in its power, mild or malignant in its indulgence, that turns the world into a battle-field of strife and blood and loads it with all its crushing weight of wounds and woe.

Dr. A. H. Strong quotes Dr. Samuel Harris as follows: "Sin is essentially egoism or selfism, putting self in God's place. It has four principal characteristics or manifestations: (1) self-sufficiency, instead of faith; (2) self-will, instead of submission; (3) self-seeking, instead of benevolence; (4) self-righteousness, instead of humility and reverence." Dr. Julius Müller, in his classic work on sin, develops this view at great length and with searching analysis. "The idol, therefore," he says, "which man, in his sin, puts in the place of God, can be no other than *his own self.* The individual self, and its gratifications, he makes the highest end of his life. His striving, in all the different forms and directions of sin, ever has self ultimately in view; the inmost nature of sin, the principle determining, and pervading it, in all its forms, is *selfishness.*"[1]

The effect of selfishness is to crowd God out of the heart and life. In heathendom it has been said that "everything was God but God himself." Heinrich Heine declared: "I am no child. I do not want a heavenly Father any more." "I celebrate myself," boasts Walt Whitman. "If I worship one thing more than another, it shall be the spread of my own body, or any part of it." The self is a devouring demon or monster that will be satisfied with nothing less than the world and the universe. "Every self, once awakened, is naturally a despot, and 'bears, like the Turk, no brother near the throne.'" Absorbing everything into itself it becomes "that man of sin, who opposeth and exalteth himself above all that is called God, or that is worshipped; so that he, as God, sitteth in the temple of God, shewing himself that he is God" (II Thess. 2: 3-4). But at the opposite pole the greatest Character of history, "existing in the form of God, counted not the being on an equality with God a thing to be grasped, but emptied himself, taking the form of a servant, being made in the likeness of men; and being in fashion as a

[1] *The Christian Doctrine of Sin,* Vol. I, p. 136. His discussion of sin as selfishness extends through pp. 131-203; and his discussion of sin as sensuousness and as finiteness through pp. 293-363.

man, he humbled himself, becoming obedient even unto death, yea, the death of the cross. Wherefore also God highly exalted him, and gave unto him the name which is above every name; that in the name of Jesus every knee should bow, of things in heaven and things under the earth, and that every tongue should confess that Jesus Christ is Lord, to the glory of God the Father" (Phil. 2:6-8).

Sin therefore is not a mere negation, the absence of good, the "silence implying sound," but a positive action of the human will and heart. It is man in the act of pulling down every throne that should rule over him and assuming and asserting his own sovereignty, as Napoleon clapped the imperial crown on his own head in Notre Dame. It is man's rebellion against every principle of right and rule of authority and usurping the very throne of God.

3. **Is Sin a State of the Soul?**—A question of great practical importance and involved in some of the deepest problems of theology is whether sin consists only in conscious volitions, or whether it also inheres in states and dispositions of the soul. There are several grounds for the view that it also resides in dispositions and states.

The disposition of the soul may be something that ought not to be, a wrong or evil in itself. It misses the mark and perverts the idea of what it should be and transgresses the law of God. It is of the nature of sin and therefore it is sin.

But it may be said that it lacks the essential element of an evil choice, the choice of a lower in the presence of a higher good. The character of the soul, however, is itself the result of choice, the accumulated deposit of countless volitions which have left each one an atom of habit in the soul and thus have slowly saturated it with evil. Character is the outgrowth of one's whole past. It is the soil that has been formed by all one's action falling into it, as the loam of the forest is formed by its own leaves. In so far as this character gives birth to our wrong choices and evil deeds, it is only giving further expression to our own free will as expressed in all these past actions. Our character is only our own free will cast and crystallized into habit and disposition, and therefore we are responsible for it.

It is the common judgment of men that the disposition may be evil in itself and a state for which men are responsible. We speak of "a bad character," and apply to the disposition all the terms of responsibility and guilt. Not only so, but we do not know how to judge one's conscious volitions and acts until we know the motives and disposition out of which they spring. If a man kills another, the moral nature of the act depends on whether he did it without malice in self-defence, or out of a murderous heart in hatred and revenge. The disposition determines the nature of the act and is as certainly guilty as the conscious act itself. In judging others we always try to go below the immediate act to the heart out of which it sprung; and an evil heart, so far from excusing, aggravates guilt. If a man were not chargeable for an evil disposition, then the worse his disposition the less blameworthy for his evil deeds would he be. On this theory the worst man would be the least guilty, and this absurdity proves the premise must be wrong. The soul makes its own disposition and must answer for it.

The deeper question whether the inherited nature is depraved and guilty belongs to theology rather than to psychology, but we may point out that human nature gives every evidence of being twisted or wrung and wrong in its constitution, and it therefore misses the mark and transgresses the law of God. It begins to show its perversity as soon as it begins to act and it calls forth the universal condemnation of men as a corrupt thing. Yet we do not regard this inherited depravity and original sin as being as heinous in its nature as sinful volitions and acquired character, and theology of various schools devises means by which undeveloped racial guilt is relieved of the consequences of sin. As a broad principle sin does not become sin for which we must answer until it receives our consent, and in the consent lies the sin.

II. A Study of Sin in Action

Having seen the psychological nature of sin, let us now look at sin in action. And at this point we cannot do better than take the record of the first temptation, as set forth in the Third Chapter of Genesis, which has never been surpassed in ethical insight and analysis and is a masterpiece of psychology.

Now the serpent was more subtle than any beast of the field which Jehovah God had made. And he said unto the woman, Yea, hath God said, Ye shall not eat of any tree of the garden? And the woman said unto the serpent, Of the fruit of the trees of the garden we may eat: but of the fruit of the tree which is in the midst of the garden, God hath said, Ye shall not eat of it, neither shall ye touch it, lest ye die. And the serpent said unto the woman, Ye shall not surely die: for God doth know that in the day ye eat thereof, then your eyes shall be opened, and ye shall be as God, knowing good and evil. And when the woman saw that the tree was good for food, and that it was a delight to the eyes, and that the tree was to be desired to make one wise, she took of the fruit thereof, and did eat; and she gave unto her husband, and he did eat (Genesis 3:1-6).

Whatever view is taken of the literary form of this narrative, its ethical truth and religious value remain the same. This temptation, while as old as the first human sin, in its essential elements is as modern as the latest sin.

This concrete instance of temptation strikingly illustrates the nature of sin as we have already discovered it The fatal act of Eve was the choice of a lower good in the presence of a higher good. The forbidden fruit was pleasant and good in itself, but in comparison and competition with the express command or the wisdom and will of God it fell infinitely below it and thereby became an evil, or wrong, or sin. It was also an act of selfishness, for by this act Eve put her own will above the will of God and her selfish gratification above the supreme good of the race.

1. **Temptation Tipped with Doubt.**—The temptation begins in a doubt suggested by Satan to the mind of Eve. The tempter approached her with the question, "Yea, hath God said, Ye shall not eat of any tree of the garden?" The question seems reasonable and innocent, and yet it cunningly conceals a poisoned suggestion; for it as much as says, "Is it possible that God would be so unjust and unkind, hard-hearted and cruel as to forbid you this innocent and good thing?" The woman unsuspectingly answered that they were permitted to eat of the fruit of the trees of the garden, but that of this particular tree God had said, "Ye shall not eat of it, neither shall ye touch it, lest ye die." Then Satan made his master stroke. He gave the lie

direct to God, declaring to the woman, "Ye shall not surely die," and went on to accuse God of denying them this tree because he knew it would make them wise, even as God himself. Eve made the fatal mistake of parleying with the tempter and listening to this evil suggestion until it got rooted in her mind and she began to have a doubt as to God's wisdom and right in forbidding her to eat of the tree. Thus the entering edge of this sin, the poisoned tip of this arrow of temptation, was doubt of God. When her faith in the absolute goodness and wisdom of God faltered ever so little she was losing her balance and was ready to slip and fall. And this is still often a first step in temptation.

Doubt sometimes has a legitimate place in our intellectual and religious life, as we shall see later, but it is also often a guilty thing and is then the first step towards a fall. A man hardly ever does a wrong thing until he at least momentarily doubts that it is wrong and persuades himself that it is right. He first doubts truth and duty. righteousness and goodness, and then he can easily see wrong things in the coloured light of his own desires. If we doubt in our hearts the fundamental verities and sanctities of life, especially if we doubt God and goodness, we have weakened our faith and courage and will in our stand against temptation and are ready to slip and slide into a lower life, if not into the ditch. "As a man thinketh in his heart, so is he." The first word of psychology against temptation is, "Keep thy heart with all diligence; for out of it are the issues of life"; especially does it bid us have deep roots of fundamental convictions that are never shaken with doubt and can stand against every storm of temptation.

2. Entrance of Temptation Through Sense Percep-

tion.—"And when the woman saw that the tree was good for food." The suggestion of the first temptation, which was distrust of God, entered through the ear-gate, and this second suggestion entered through the eye-gate. All our senses are so many gates which are being assailed by a constant series of assaults; for as a temptation may be a good thing in competition with a higher good, all the countless sounds, sights, and other sensations that are ceaselessly pouring in upon us are possible temptations.

The human body is a marvellous mechanism of nerves, a harp of a million strings, and it is played upon by all the impacts upon the senses that set it vibrating in sensation. These sensations kindle in the soul ideas and feelings, desires and passions, and may set it aflame with pleasure or consume it in agony. And thus a sight or a sound, perhaps incidentally and accidentally caught on the wing, a mere flake of sensation that lights on us as we pass along, a face at a window, a whiff of odour or a strain of music floating out of an open door, a gleam of gold in a purse or the flash of a jewel on a hand, a mere word heard in a crowd, any sensation, however trivial and insignificant it may seem, may start a suggestion that tempts us, be the spark that kindles the evil nature in our hearts. And as our sensations are our most vivid and vital forms of knowledge, they cut into the very quick of the soul and draw blood, they sway us at times with sovereign power as tornadoes sweep their way through forest and city. The man with a craving for strong drink is in the grip of his appetite, the odour of the saloon as he passes by is a match to the tinder of his desire, and he is almost irresistibly taken captive by his sense of smell and becomes its pitiful victim.

And the senses are inlets, not only to temptations of sensual gratification, but also to the more refined and spiritual temptations of the soul. Ambition and pride were kindled in Eve by the suggestion of the fruit that could make her wise, and the world in all its millionfold aspects of wealth and power, position and influence, is appealing to our ambition and vanity and selfishness and dropping sparks of spiritual temptation into our hearts. Our souls are highly sensitive and absorbent to these things to which we are constantly exposed. Like men carrying packages of powder through a burning building we are loaded with explosive materials in our natures while we walk through a flaming world showering sparks upon us from every side. That the world should be so constituted may seem to us a terrible mystery and tragedy, but this is its stern reality.

3. **Association Intensifies Temptation.**—We next see how the first suggestion of temptation is intensified by association. The woman's mind immediately began to multiply associations around the forbidden fruit and to enhance its attractiveness. She "saw that the tree was good for food, and that it was a delight to the eyes, and that the tree was to be desired to make one wise": three powerful suggestions giving accumulated charm and force to the temptation. "Good for food,"—sin always presents itself as good, clothes itself as an angel of light, and hardly ever does one deliberately do a wrong until he has found some justification for it and persuaded himself it is right and good.

And it was "a delight to the eyes,"—it was not only good but also beautiful, an appeal to her esthetic nature. Sin is not always coarse but may be something fine. The artistic nature in us is a fine-stringed harp capable of exquisite music, one of the great joys of the world, but it is also a source of danger and may be full of discord and tragedy, as all the history of art and artists shows.

And " to be desired to make one wise,"—this is something higher and finer still. It is an appeal to the intellectual and moral nature, to the thirst for knowledge that has driven the human mind to such high endeavours and grand achievements, and to the very search for wisdom that leads the soul deepest into the meaning of life and closest to the will of God.

Thus the mind and imagination of Eve played around and brooded over this forbidden thing. It multiplied in her mind rich and alluring associations and kindled ever stronger desires, hushed all the voices of duty and danger and fear, lulled into a deeper sleep her sense of obligation to God, laid an ever more fascinating and fatal spell on her senses, until it obsessed her whole soul and she was ready for the decisive deed. This is the psychology of all deliberate sin. It is a growth. It begins with a sense perception or with an idea which attracts to itself all the kindred associations of the mind that enrich and strengthen it; it weaves around itself a web of witchery, it crowds its guilt and fatal consequences into the background and hides all its repulsive features in a halo of light, it roots itself in the whole heart, and thus it decides and moves the will. The devil is a master psychologist and knows how to play on all the complex strings and keys of the human heart.

And this suggests the way to resist temptation. The inhibitory ideas and associations must be aroused and rushed to the rescue. Lying around on the margin of the mind in a more or less dim and dormant state are various ideas and feelings that are opposed to the central idea that is the temptation. Just at this point lies our chief power and responsibility. We can turn our attention to these marginal ideas and intensify them so that they will take the centre of consciousness and crowd out the evil thought. If Eve had fixed her mind on the duty of loyalty to God and of trusting his wisdom and will, however strange and even unkind and cruel it seemed; if she had considered the danger that lurked in that forbidden fruit so that she would have seen that its rosy glow was as the hectic flush of a deadly fever or the gleaming fires of hell; if she had pictured the possible consequences of disobedience and seen the flaming sword shutting her from the garden, she would, like Jesus in the wilderness, have resisted the devil until he would have fled into the darkness whence he came.

The tempted soul can always arouse and marshal opposing ideas, fears of consequences and feelings of loyalty and right and duty, and thus check the insurgent temptation and drive it from the centre of attention and out of the field of consciousness. Association is just as strong a power for good as it is for evil. It can weave webs of fascination and paint pictures that will make good look attractive and evil repulsive. And when association has deep roots of faith and the fruitage of a rich mind and good life to draw from, it can marshal such forces of character and resolution as will conquer spiritual hosts of wickedness, "casting down imaginations, and every high thing that is exalted against the knowledge of God, and bringing every thought into captivity to the obedience of Christ." This is the victory that overcomes the world.

4. **The Act of Sin.**—This brings us to the decisive

act and deed of sin. " She took of the fruit thereof, and did eat." *She* did this deed. Satan did not do it for her, and the tree did not do it, the garden did not do it, her environment and circumstances did not do it, and God did not do it. And it was not her heredity that led her to do this deed, and it was not even the pleasant associations that enriched the fruit with goodness and beauty and charm that did it, but "*she* took thereof, and did eat." This deed was her own personal, individual, wilful, responsible act, and the blame of it must rest on her forever.

And so is it with every sinner and every sin. Whatever conditions of heredity and birth, training and opportunity, whatever means and motives entered into it, whatever the depraved disposition out of which it sprung, every sin is the sinner's own personal responsible act, and he cannot roll the blame of it on anybody or anything else. Of course heredity and disposition and training and circumstances do enter into and modify the degree of guilt. No two men are any more alike in their inner nature than in their outer circumstances, in their sin than in their saintliness; yet every soul commits its own sin and must bear the burden of its own guilt. " So then each of us shall give account of himself to God."

The tendency is strong in our day to tone down the guilt of sin and resolve it into heredity and environment, or to roll it upon the social order. Bad heredity is supposed to foreordain a man to a criminal career, and the social order is held responsible for all human sins. If we were only all born of pure blood and especially if we were only placed in a just and good and beautiful social order in which we would all have comfortable homes and fine clothes and plenty to eat and little to do, we would all be good. But the history of this first sin does not bear out this rosy view. There was nothing wrong with the heredity of Eve, and the pleasant garden did not save her from falling into sin: rather it was the very occasion and temptation of her sin. All human history shows that increase of wealth is not in itself a safeguard of virtue, but is often a rank soil out which grow scarlet sins of the vilest rottenness and deepest guilt. A bad social order aggravates human ill and evil and every effort should be made to correct it, but it is not the real root and cause of human sin. Bad environment does not make evil souls so much as evil souls make bad environment. The soul is not the slave of its circumstances, but is rather their master and sits upon its own throne.

We are here face to face with the fact of the sovereignty of the human soul over its ethical life. As we have already seen, the contents of consciousness, its sense perceptions, ideas, memories, feelings, associations, are not an ungovernable flood on which the will floats rudderless and helpless, but the soul has its own rudder and engine by which it can steer and drive its boat to its own destination. It can throw its attention upon any point in its consciousness, as a searchlight can be thrown around the horizon, and wherever it falls and is fixed the idea under its light blazes up into vividness and glowing heat and power and becomes the controlling centre of the mind and life. Eve chose to magnify the attractive associations of the forbidden fruit, instead of choosing to intensify its hidden sting and poison and to emphasize and deepen her sense of the goodness and beauty and blessedness of obedience to God; and essentially the same psychological process takes place in every sinner in the act of sin. The soul has various competitive objects in its field of consciousness, some of which it knows are of higher worth and obligation than others; it always has the power of making its choice and fixing its attention upon one rather than upon another, and then of multiplying and enhancing its associations and motives until they carry the will as with a flood into decision and action. This is the inescapable point of human responsibility. Psychology is severely orthodox at this point and fixes the guilt of sin on the sinner himself.

5. **The Sense of Sin.**—The act of sin in an unseared conscience is followed by the sense of sin. Immediately after the first sin " the eyes of them both were opened," and they were aware of their physical and moral nakedness. A sense of guilt filled them with fear and they hid in the garden of the Lord from the Lord of the garden.

Sin seizes the soul with a sense of its guilt and vileness and degradation. The purer the soul the deeper and keener this sense of the wrong and bitterness of sin. Often the act of sin is instantly followed with an awful sense of guilt and remorse. The soul may agonize and cry out in despair. But this sense of guilt becomes hardened through repeated acts of sin until conscience is seared and hardened and guilt almost ceases to be felt.

The sense of sin varies as widely in its forms and feelings as individual souls differ in their constitution and temperament and in all the circumstances of their temptation and fall. Professor E. D. Starbuck made an inductive study of " preconversion " experience by sending out a list of questions to about two hundred persons asking for personal details in the matter and then tabulating the answers. He summarizes the result as follows: "There are many shades of experience in the preconversion state. An attempt at classification of them gave these not very distinct groups:—Conviction of sin proper; struggle after the new life; prayer, calling on God; doubts and questionings; tendency to resist conviction; depression and sadness; restlessness, anxiety and uncertainty; helplessness and humility; earnestness and seriousness; and the various bodily affections. The result of an analysis of these different shades of experience coincides with the common designation of this preconversion state in making the *central fact in it all the sense of sin, while the other conditions are various manifestations of this, as determined, first, by differences in temperament, and, second, by whether the ideal life or the sinful life is vivid in consciousness*. . . . The cases arrange themselves pretty naturally in two series. In the first place, they form a series as determined by temperament. There are those at one end of the line, who are thrown back on themselves, and who remain helpless, depressed and estranged from God. At the other extreme are those who reach out in the direction of the new life, who strive toward it, and pray toward it, or, if the forces which awaken the impulse toward the higher life have dawned unawares and in spite of themselves, they wilfully oppose the new influences. Between these two extremes are those who are eminently conscious of sin, but remain poised in a state of restlessness and anxiety, or who vacillate between activity and passivity. This temperamental series, that is, ranges all the way from persons, on the one hand, who are passive, to those, on the other, who are active and positive." [1]

The various experiences of sin may also be viewed or

[1] *The Psychology of Religion*, pp. 58-59.

classified with reference to the dominant object on which the sense of it fastens itself. This object may be the sinner's self as he is conscious of having violated his own sense of right and dignity and self-respect, of having polluted his own purity and marred his own worth. He is conscious of having lost his own soul, and this sting may go deep and inflict great suffering. Or the sense of sin may fasten on the fellow-man whom the sinner has wronged. The offender is then conscious of having invaded and violated the rights of another and of having wronged him in his person or property or reputation, or of having stained and corrupted his soul, and this fills him with regret and remorse.

The sense of sin, however, when it follows out its logical implications and incidences, runs up against God as the first and the final object of its transgression and wrong. The soul is conscious of having violated his law of truth and right and of having offended his justice and goodness and grace. This sense of sin against God ranges in directness and degree from a faint conception and feeling of " uneasiness in the presence of the higher powers," to revert to Professor James's phrase, to the intense consciousness that the offence against God swallows up all other aspects and consequences of sin, and the penitent soul cries out, " Against thee, thee only, have I sinned, and done evil in thy sight."

The sense of sin may also predominately fasten itself on some special idea or aspect of it. It may be conscious chiefly of its pollution, its wrong, its guilt, its remorse, or its retribution. Its pollution is the stain with which sin spoils the purity and beauty of the soul and corrupts it with its vileness. Its wrong is the fact that the soul fell below its own sense of value and obligation and chose a lower in the presence of a higher good. Its guilt is the sense of having violated the law and justice of God so as to be responsible to him. The remorse of sin is its "biting" the soul, as the word means, gnawing at its very vitals with distress and intolerable pain. The retribution of sin is the penalty paid back by it to justice as its due return. The enlightened soul may have a deep sense that its sin violates the justice of God and owes to it the satisfaction of its own penalty and pain.

This aspect of sin runs into the question of why punishment for sin is inflicted and endured, a point that goes deep into government both human and divine and may determine our doctrine of the atonement. One theory is that punishment is inflicted only as a reforming and deterrent instrument in its influence on the offender and on others. Of course punishment does have this effect, and this is one of its incidental objects; but it is not its direct and main end. The direct ground of punishment is the ill desert of sin and its direct object is the satisfaction of the justice it has violated. This is intuitively perceived and felt by the conscience as the ultimate fact in the nature of law and justice. To punish a man to deter him or others from wrong acts not yet committed is itself an act of injustice. It is doing wrong in the hope that right may result, evil that good may come, and this is a self-contradictory principle that never can be justified. Punishment is just only when it is inflicted as the due desert of sin, and then it may act as a reforming and deterring influence on the individual and in society as its indirect result and aim.

Instances are not infrequent of men that have committed sin, which was covered up and forgotten, and that afterwards led lives of respectability and success. But the hidden sin kept burrowing and gnawing deep in their souls, burning them as a pent-up fire and tormenting them as flames of hell. A sense of their guilt and just desert of retribution gave them no rest, until at length they unbosomed themselves in public confession and not only exposed their guilt but asked and demanded punishment as their just retribution and satisfaction to human and divine justice. The human heart is tremendously orthodox at this point and often insists on paying the price and penalty of sin, however bitter it may be.

Literature bears abundant witness to this solemn fact. Victor Hugo gives a memorable instance of it in Jean Valjean. Greek tragedy voices its inexorability, fiction and poetry, drama and painting portray it in powerful forms and vivid colours, and from a cross on Calvary floats a voice declaring, in the agony of death, "And we indeed justly; for we receive the due reward of our deeds." Retributive justice is an essential element in the divine nature, a foundation stone of the throne of the universe. "Be not deceived; God is not mocked: for whatsoever a man soweth, that shall he also reap."

6. The Enslavement and Contagion of Sin.—Sin follows the law of habit. A wrong choice tends to repeat itself. An evil deed leaves a network of associations in the mind, and on the next occasion of temptation this network revives its tendency and power and lures or drags the soul back into the same deed. Repetition grows into a habit, and one habit associates itself with others and grows into a system of habits or character. Evil acts and habits also react on the nature of the soul, leaving a deposit of evil in the heart, and this process goes on until the whole soul is stained and saturated with evil and hardened into an evil disposition. Conscience slowly loses its sensitiveness and becomes seared and can in time consent to the wickedest or vilest deeds without compunction. Men thus become "wise to do evil," "hardened sinners," and "dead in trespasses and sins."

As every one sees the world through his own soul so that he sees things not only as they are but also as he is, when one is soaked and corrupted with any form of evil, such as avarice or lust, everything stirs this evil nature in him, and finally he sees the whole glorious universe, which to the good and beautiful soul is only a scene of divine purity and splendour, as a hideous mass of corruption.

The soul is thus enslaved in bondage that may be more binding and bitter than prison bars or slave-driver's lash. The worst master any one can have over him is an evil disposition within him. A spirit of consuming egoism and selfishness, or of irritability and evil temper, or of suspicion and jealousy and hatred and malice, blinds and binds the soul as in a prison cell. Evil habits become the most galling chains that strong crying and tears cannot break. No slavery is so dreadful as that of a nature saturated with sin and bound with evil habit. Many a man beats against the prison bars of his own soul and cries out in his despair, "O wretched man that I am! who shall deliver me from the body of this death?" And yet this terrible imprisonment does not excuse him from responsibility for his condition, for it is the outgrowth and fruitage of his repeated acts of free choice, and he is simply eating of the fruit of his own doings.

While sin is enslaving to the self it is also contagious

to others. The woman "gave also unto her husband, and he did eat." And Adam, having caught the infection, immediately showed the working of sin in himself. He became adept at excusing himself and blaming somebody else. "And the man said, The woman whom thou gavest to be with me, she gave me of the tree, and I did eat." He took fifteen words to tell what the woman had done and only three words to tell what he had done. The self-deception of sin at once began to blind the soul, and the art of blaming others was born full-grown and expert into the world. Thus the contagion of sin infected the race at the fountain head and started its virus coursing down the veins of all succeeding generations.

That sin is catching is one of the most obvious facts of the world. The human soul is intensely social and absorbent and readily gives and receives both good and evil. An evil state in one heart begets a like evil state in another heart by a process of induction or suggestion. Language is a living stream of communication which transmits thoughts, feelings, states and deeds and habits from one person to another; and all actions, gestures, tones of the voice, play of the features and glances of the eye are subtle channels of transmission from one soul to another. The whole contents of the soul may thus pour in a flood into another soul and fill it with its good or evil. A word, a touch, an expression of the face or eye may be the infection by which one soul poisons and pollutes another. All social institutions and means of instruction recognize this contagion of evil, and many precepts and proverbs in all languages warn against it. "Evil communications corrupt good manners." We warn our children against evil companions and try to guard them against all evil infection. Particular kinds of evil may run in families, or communities, or races, and some families, such as the "Jukes" family, have become notorious for the bad character transmitted and bred from generation to generation. Evil gravitates to and generates in the slums of cities, and particular places become breeding grounds and plague spots of sin and crime. Saloons and dens of vice are pests that spread their evil contagion abroad and poison whole neighbourhoods and infect the very air.

Thus sin is a terrible power that enslaves the sinner and a highly contagious disease that spreads through society and has infected the whole of humanity. The prophet Isaiah's diagnosis of his own nation applies to all the world: "Ah, sinful nation, a people laden with iniquity, a seed of evil-doers, children that are corrupters! . . . From the sole of the foot even unto the head there is no soundness in it; but wounds, and bruises, and putrifying sores" (Isaiah 1:4, 6).

III. Is the Sense of Sin Declining?

This question is usually answered in the affirmative. The pulpit proclaims the fact of such decline, religious newspapers and magazines publish it, and people generally affirm and feel it. What can be said as to this evident change?

1. **Abatement of the General Sense of Fear.**—There has been an abatement of the general sense of fear. In ancient times it was believed that the world swarmed with evil demons that lurked in every object, waiting and watching to seize their human victims. They infested every forest, hovered over every path and hid behind or within every stone, and were the cause of dis-

ease and of every disaster, such as fire and flood, and of every individual misfortune. This is still the prevailing belief among primitive people, such as savages, and in some heathen countries, such as China, and it fills the world with fears and makes life a constant terror. Science has swept these demons out of the world and made it a safe place. It has also removed or relieved many other fears, such as witches and ghosts, and has cleared up the apparent confusion and caprice of nature into law and order. All this has greatly abated fear and increased the sense of security and life has lost much of its mystery and dread.

This decline of fear in general has had some effect in abating the fear of sin. Men have connected religious fear with these fears that have vanished and think that it may be only another false alarm and not so serious after all. They may feel that it is a childish weakness to fear sin and declare that they refuse to be caught and cowed by this religious ghost.

> Beyond this place of wrath and tears
>   Looms but the Horror of the shade,
> And yet the menace of the years
>   Finds and shall find me unafraid.

Yet on what meat have men been feeding that they have grown so great as to outgrow fear? Do they not still fear fire and flood and disease and is not fear a fundamental fact and safeguard of our life at a thousand points? And if we experience and are governed by fear on the lower levels of life, why not on the higher? If human justice is a true ground of fear to evil-doers, is there not an infinitely greater ground to fear the justice and judgment of Almighty God? There is much to justify the general abatement of fear and this has relieved our life of much terror and has blessed it, but we go too far and rebound to an opposite extreme and will surely run into ruin if we eliminate the fear of sin and treat it as a light thing. "The fear of the Lord is the beginning of wisdom."

2. Reaction Against Extreme Views of Hell.—There has been a decided reaction against extreme views of hell. The old view of hell was that it was a literal lake or furnace of fire in which the lost forever burned and raved in physical agony. The horrible scenes portrayed in Dante's *Inferno* expressed the literal belief of the Middle Ages, and the terrible illustrations supplied to the poem by Doré have given further expression to the same view. This doctrine has passed out of our theology and preaching. It is not supported by a true understanding of Scripture and is intolerable to our views of God. Reaction against one extreme nearly always swings to another, and this has taken place at this point. The flames of hell have almost died out in the pulpit. Only sensational evangelists now preach them in lurid rhetoric, and even they are not taken seriously by the audiences that listen to them with scarcely concealed incredulity and with lightness of mind that in the midst of such discourses is ready to ripple into a smile or break into laughter.

This change in the form in which the doctrine of future punishment is held and preached has undoubtedly abated the sense of sin. Men do not fear spiritual retribution as they did literal flames. The modern hell is sometimes represented as a quite tolerable if not a comfortable and respectable place, and men are not inclined to take it seriously. In passing from one form of a doctrine to another there is always danger of losing something in the transition, and it takes time to realize that a spiritual hell may be as terrible as a lake of fire.

3. **Changed Views of the Character of God.**—Changed views of the character of God have also affected our sense of sin. The old theology and modes of preaching painted God in terrible colours. In his famous sermon on " Sinners in the Hands of an Angry God," Jonathan Edwards addresses sinners in the following language: " The God that holds you over the pit of hell much as one holds a spider or some loathsome insect over the fire, abhors you, and is dreadfully provoked; His wrath towards you burns like fire; He looks upon you as worthy of nothing else but to be cast into the fire; He is of purer eyes than to bear you in His sight; you are ten thousand times as abominable in His eyes, as the most hateful and venomous serpent is in ours." Jonathan Edwards believed in the literal reality of this dreadful picture and his audience believed in it, and this fact gave the sermon its terrible power. People cried out and fell down upon the floor under its awful judgments. But such a sermon would not be preached in any enlightened Christian pulpit to-day. It is a libel on God. A change of climate has come over our views of God and we think of him as the Father of our spirits and a God of mercy and love.

The modern view is nearer Scripture teaching and is truer to the God and Father of our Lord Jesus Christ, but like other reactions against extremes it is in danger of going too far and giving us a soft and indulgent Father who will not deal with sin severely. According to this conception, God is too kind and courteous to hurt us, too polite to punish us. Some hold that " God is too good to punish sinners and sinners are too go to be punished," and any such view will greatly weaken the sense of sin. Huxley revolted against the soft sentiment which "represents Providence under the guise of a paternal philanthropist" and thought the old theologians were "vastly nearer the truth than the 'liberal' popular illusions" because they "recognize the realities of things."[1]

4. **Changed Views of Sin Itself.**—Sin itself has received some explanations that explain it away. One such theory denies the fact of sin outright, and declares that it is wholly a delusion of the mind and that the simple way to get rid of it is to forget it. This theory goes to pieces on the sharp and terrible rocks of reality. Any pantheistic or deterministic theory of the world cuts up sin by the roots and reduces it to pure mechanism and necessity so that it is no more a guilty choice and act than the growth of grass or the fall of a stone, and such views have been popularized in much of our literature. Socialism is predominately materialistic and deterministic in its underlying philosophy and it is being widely diffused. Many have also largely resolved sin into heredity and environment and a wrong social order. Man is doomed to be bad by his bad birth. Society soaks his soul in the slums, and how, then, can it expect him to be good? Unjust poverty and the dire necessity of hunger drive men to lie and steal and thereby render virtue a physical impossibility. Adam blamed his sin on Eve, Eve blamed it on the serpent, and thus was started this theory of rolling sin off on the environment and the social order. Sin thus becomes a misfortune and not a fault, and the sinner is a victim and not an offender. He has not done wrong, but wrong has been done to him. He does not owe

[1] See *The World a Spiritual System*, p. 277.

penitence to God, but God owes him an apology. As Omar Kháyyám expresses it:

> O Thou, who Man of Baser Earth didst make,
> And even with Paradise devise a Snake,
> For all the Sin wherewith the Face of Man
> Is blackened—Man's forgiveness give—and take!

Or as poor James Thomson in his "City of Dreadful Night" expresses it more boldly if not blasphemously:

> Who is most wretched in this dolorous place?
> I think myself; yet I would rather be
> My miserable self than He, than He
> Who formed such creatures to His own disgrace.

These pantheistic and deterministic views have percolated deeply and widely through our literature and life, and more than any other cause they have weakened our sense of sin.

The counteractive to this error is the appeal to and affirmation of our intuitional conscience in our immediate and ineradicable sense of free agency and responsibility and guilt in connection with our sin, a responsibility that is affirmed in all the laws and is reflected in all the literature of the world and that rolls its solemn voice through all the ages.

5. **Our Modern Life Less Subjective and More Objective.**—There has been in our day a marked change in the nature of our life. In former days life was more introspective and subjective. People were more conscious of themselves and grew meditative and morbid. They looked within and worked much with their inwards. They indulged much in self-examination. They held fast days when they shut out the world, reduced their bodily life to its lowest limits, and intensified

their consciousness of their souls. Sin was a dominant fact in this introspection, the burning centre of their self-consciousness. They deepened and darkened their sense of guilt and agonized over their sin. Religious literature was largely devotional and meditative, and such books as Bunyan's *Pilgrim's Progress,* Jeremy Taylor's *Holy Living* and his *Holy Dying,* Baxter's *Saints' Everlasting Rest*, and Doddridge's *Rise and Progress of Religion in the Soul* were the popular religious books of their day. The preaching partook of the same character and turned the gaze of the hearers inward upon their own spiritual condition.

Our life has become predominantly objective. We live in a unified world which has become a vast amphitheatre where the drama of humanity is being played before our eyes. We all hold reserved seats in this theatre and see all that is going on. Book and daily newspaper and illustrated magazine, telephone and telegraph and wireless communication, have brought the ends of the earth together, and everything of any importance and countless things of no importance happening anywhere are thrown on the screen before us in a moving-picture show that is giving a continuous performance. As a result we are absorbed in our senses. The heavens are full of shooting stars and, while looking at one wonder, we are distracted by another. We have little time and disposition to look within because of the great, chaotic, noisy, booming world without. We live in a riot of the senses and are too excited to think. Our literature is emotional and sensational, and our newspapers scream at us in red-letter headlines from two to four inches deep. Even the pulpit in many instances turns itself into a platform on which some kind of a performance is going on to draw and hold an audience, and travelling evangelists take to extemporized tents and tabernacles in which the wildest sensationalism is often the chief attraction.

Meditation is thus becoming a lost art. People are always craving a crowd and itching for a new thrill. They seek excitement in society and shun solitude. They have meagre inner resources and little comfort and contentment in themselves. We are losing acquaintance with ourselves and may become such strangers to our own souls that we would hardly recognize them on the street. In such a world, to which we are not yet adjusted, we are losing much that is valuable and fine out of our inner life, and our sense of sin is being submerged and swept away in this flood of external excitement.

There is much that is good in this objective life, but we are swinging to a dangerous extreme and need to return to and restore the inner life. The inner must balance the outer, or life will lack depth and proportion and poise, and be one-sided and shallow, feverish and fretful. There must be inner roots of conviction deepened by self-examination and meditation in order that there may be a strong and fruitful outer life. The Delphic oracle was wise enough to enjoin upon the seeker after the secret of life, "Know thyself." and we are in special need of the same admonition and practice in our day. Such self-knowledge will bring us face to face with our sin and convince and convict us of our guilt and drive the sense of sin deep into our souls.

6. Increased Emphasis on the Positive Side of Life. —Increased emphasis is now being placed on the positive side of life. There are two ways of controlling ourselves and moving men to action: the negative way of checks and fears, and the positive way of active impulses and hopes. The one intensifies inhibitory ideas and motives, and the other stresses positive motives and ends. The one cries out, "Woe to the wicked; it shall be ill with him"; and the other proclaims, "Say ye to the righteous, that it shall be well with him." The one holds back, and the other draws forward. The one emphasizes retribution, and the other holds up reward. The one points to hell, and the other to heaven. Both of these means and motives are proper and should be used in their due proportion.

Now in former days the chief stress was put on restraint and fear, but in our day it has shifted to action and hope. Men are now more aroused and governed by hope than by fear, by reward than by retribution. They want to be energized to do something positive and not simply checked and held back. They are lured and inspired by great visions that can be turned into victories and have small concern simply in avoiding danger and disaster, even the traps of Satan and the pit of hell.

The preaching of to-day reflects this changed attitude. Its dominant emphasis is put upon positive doctrine and deeds rather than upon negative restraints. It preaches the great things of the gospel, the personality and character of God, the Saviourhood of Christ, the greatness of the kingdom of God, the worth of life, the blessedness of service and sacrifice, and the crown of life that fadeth not away. Of course the guilt and ruin and bitter fruits of sin are also preached, as they ought to be, but the purity and peace and power of righteousness are preached more. Salvation is made to overshadow sin, and good to crowd out evil. Men can be interested more in doing right than in not doing wrong. They are urged to gird themselves up as strong men to run a race, not to escape enemies, but to win a prize. This is good psychology, for the way to get evil out of the soul is to crowd good in, but this change has had the effect in some degree of drawing our consciousness off from sin and concentrating it on righteousness.

7. **A Broader and Finer Ethical Sense.**—The picture on which we have been looking is growing less dark and increasingly taking on brighter colours. In the midst of these ominous conditions and changes we are developing a broader and finer ethical sense. While some things that in former days were regarded as deep sins, such as dancing, cards, and the theatre, are losing their darker aspects and are fading out into general tolerance if not acceptance among Christian people, other things that former generations did not consider wrong are now pressing on our conscience as grave social sins. Slavery, once thought right and even defended as a divine institution, is now branded as "the sum of all villainies." Gambling, once a gentleman's game, is now banished from most respectable circles. Intemperance, once indulged in without social or religious disapproval, is now a grave sin and scandal.

Significant also is the growth of conscience in the political, business and industrial worlds. Politics is undoubtedly subject to higher ethical standards than in former days and is growing cleaner and more honourable. Public opinion appears to be growing purer and more powerful. Business and industrial legislation is making constant progress along ethical lines. Railroad rebates, given or extorted only a generation ago without any one questioning them, are now prohibited by law as social crimes. Monopolies and trusts are also now regarded as unjust and are forbidden by law. A great body of legislation is growing up regulating child labour, the labour of women, the hours of labour, protection from dangerous machinery and unsanitary conditions, compensation for injuries and related matters, all of which mark and measure progress in social conscience. While individual conscience at some points is growing less tender, social conscience is growing more sensitive and imperative.

The sense of truth is growing finer and more exacting. We feel more the obligation to reach reality at any cost and not be governed by tradition or public opinion or partisan or personal interest. The church is being held to stricter account for the character and conduct of its members, and there is an increasing insistence that Christian profession be matched with practice. The scientific spirit of truth-seeking is pervading the intellectual realm and the Christian spirit of brotherhood is being diffused through social life from top to bottom.

Broader and more hopeful still, there is developing a world consciousness and a world conscience. The world, once broken into dissevered and constantly warring fragments, has grown into unity and is forming a court of world morality in which its ethical sense is steadily moving up the scale of worth and obligation. Humanity is beginning to realize its brotherhood and to speak on international questions with a majestic voice. And this is true in the face of the present world war, which is giving a mighty impulse to the growing world consciousness and conscience, and which may be one of the last dreadful convulsions of the whole insanity of war. At any rate, there is a growing conscience against war which was scarcely felt five centuries or even one century ago, and the world appears to be moving towards the long dreamed-of " parliament of man and federation of the world." And thus conscience is developing a broader and finer sense, and this immensely hopeful fact is to be placed to the credit side of this account.

8. The Terrible Fact of Sin Remains.—The final fact on this subject is that notwithstanding the sense of sin has declined at some points and in some ways, the terrible reality of sin remains. Some of these conditions that have dulled the sense of sin are reactions against the extremes of other days, and the pendulum is bound to swing back and rest nearer to the normal middle position; others are less serious than they seem, and still others are a positive gain. But in and through them all the fact of sin has not been removed or shaken. The soul is aware of its own transgression and guilt and all the multitudinous seas cannot wash out this stain. No self-deception can permanently blind the soul to its guilt, no false theory can explain it away. Conscience cries out against itself, and its voice cannot be hushed. Sin is still a frightful fact in the world. It writes its ruin in vice and crime, in individual murder and in the colossal convulsions of war, in all human selfishness and cruelty, trials and tears, sufferings and sorrows, broken hearts and lost souls. It is the awful tragedy of the universe. Only fools mock at it. Angels weep over it, and the Son of God gave himself as a sacrifice to atone for its guilt. Its retribution cannot be escaped. Hell cannot be dug out of the universe or its fires be put out. God's justice never slumbers or sleeps. He cannot overlook sin and be a respectable God. The integrity of the universe will not tolerate it. God will not let it mock him, and it is still an eternal law of life that the wages of sin is death.

We should not, then, let our sense of sin be lulled into indifference and dulness and drowsiness, but we should arouse it and keep it alive and alert, and the prophets and preachers of the age should cry aloud and spare not.